DATING 'n'
MATING

Wit and Wisdom on
Love and Marriage

DATING 'n' MATING

CONNIE JAMESON

For information about this title or to order other books
and/or electronic media, contact the publisher:

Gray Fox
grayfox44@protonmail.com

ISBNs:
978-1-954303-00-3 (print)
978-1-954303-01-0 (eBook)

Printed in the United States of America

Cover and interior design: 1106 Design

Dedicated to Tom

"#1 Husband"

"Perfect 10"

Thanks for providing lots of "material."

TABLE OF CONTENTS

Husbands . . . The "Expert" Speaks

Playing the Dating Game

"Tying the Knot" and Beyond

More Thoughts on Love

HUSBANDS...

The "Expert" Speaks

HUSBANDS

Husband #1

My husband, the First
Oh, he was the worst

> Dashing, dapper, a real dandy
> To all the girls, he was "eye candy"

I didn't worry. Everything was fine
'Cause Mr. Handsome—he was all mine
Until he wasn't

> Started to stray, started to roam
> That's when he lost his happy home

Told that Rover
"So long—it's over!"

Husband #2

Husband Number Two
Oh, Boo Hoo! Boo Hoo!

> You'd think I would have learned
> But, no—again, I got burned

Fell for the sexy smile, the bedroom eyes
Oh, how they could hypnotize!

> Yes, I came under his Magic Spell
> As did many other girls as well

So, Mr. Romeo—farewell, farewell!

Husband #3

For choice of Husband Number Three
You'd be so very proud of me

> No longer would I emphasize looks
> I'd choose a man who was into—books!

Quiet evenings sharing a novel or two
You read to me, I'll read to you

> Discussions of authors and poets—Oh, boy!
> I'd know them all—Shakespeare, Tolstoy . . .

Books large and books small
Together, we'd devour them all

> But I tired of "Book Guy" and sent him out
>   the door
> So I could start searching for . . . Husband
>   Number Four

Husband #4

Because Mr. Bookworm became such a bore
I had a new plan for Husband Number Four

> I'd find an athlete, an outdoors man
> Yes, he would be a #1 Sports Fan

The problem that I didn't see
Was that he liked his sports, but—on *TV*!

> It felt like I wasn't even there
> As buddies filled every couch and chair

Wait it out, be patient, I tried to think
As I brought them all more beer to drink

> Surely this would have to end
> (TV Remote was now his best friend)

But, no, there are sports in every season
So that, my friends, became the reason

> I said, "Bye, Bye,
> Mr. Sports Guy!"

Husband #5

Land Sakes, Alive!
I couldn't believe it—Husband Number *Five*!

> This new husband, a *true* athlete, hiker, runner
> After "TV sports guy," I knew he'd be much
>   "funner"

Together we'd hike and trek over trail, valley, and hill
Of good ol' outdoor exercise, we would have our fill

> Oh, I had *my* fill—of blisters, pains, and aches
> "Stop, please stop. Stop, for goodness sakes!"

He couldn't stop—he was a hiking *fanatic*
So now I knew that I would have to pick

> My mind said, "Yes," but my body said, "No!"
> So, sadly, Mr. Athlete would have to go

Husband #6

I really hoped that Number Six
Would be my husband-problem fix

> Of course, he should
> He was just plain—*good*

So nice, polite, attentive, just swell
And made my life a living hell

> Why? *Too* agreeable, *too* pampering—boring!
> He was vanilla, milquetoast, a big Nothing!

Like one of those Bobble Heads—up, down, up, down
Always a painted-on smile—never, ever a frown

> I grew tired, couldn't take it anymore
> So I shoved "Sweet Guy" out the door

Husband #7

With Husband Number Seven
I envisioned Culinary Heaven

> Could it possibly be?
> He wants to cook for me!

He was not exactly "fit as a fiddle"
Sporting extra inches around the middle

> But, hey, that was okay
> He'd be making gourmet meals all day

Turns out he didn't like to cook—just bake
Every sort of cookie, pie, and cake

> Problem was he spent all day
> Worrying about his dumb soufflé!

Told him, "One more *petit four*
And I am out the door"

> My cute little "Dough Boy" in his white baker's hat
> Can you believe it? He did just that

Baked more biscuits, fritters, and muffins
So I left him in the kitchen—"lovin' his oven"

Husband #8

Swept off my feet by Husband Number Eight
I knew that he would be absolutely great

> Plus, he'd help rid me of what I'd found
> Courtesy of "Baker Man"—extra pounds!

Yes, I'd shed those extra pounds and more
As Dance Instructor twirled me round the floor

> It'd be Cha, Cha, Cha and Two to Tango
> Do a little tap dance and on to the Fandango

Ballroom floor—what a place to exercise
Then cool down with a waltz and gaze into his eyes

> Head on his shoulder, sweet nothings in my ear
> *But this can't last forever*, I started to fear

I was right—
Because one night

> After private lessons, when he'd glide, swirl,
>   and twirl
> His prize pupil—beautiful ballerina (former
>   can-can girl!)

He didn't return to me
So our dance is over, as you can see

Husband #9

Husband Number Nine
Another Einstein

> So full of wisdom and knowledge
> Esteemed professor at the college

His specialty—physics, of the quantum kind
The smartest brainiac one could find

> Certificates and PhDs filled every wall and shelf
> I hoped I'd gain a little of that smartness for myself

My professor's intellect was really quite superb
I was so impressed, hung on his every word

> A walking encyclopedia was what he seemed to me
> So, what I learned next, I just couldn't believe

Shocking—a man with so much knowledge to impart
Would be "educating" some college co-ed (the little tart!)

> Well, I sent that Professor out the door
> Arms stacked full of books, degrees, and more

Husband #10

Oh, no! Husband Number Ten!
What a tangled web I'm in!

>This scary trend
>Must surely end

Here and now!
Just tell me how

>Should I quit "cold turkey," as they say
>Just give up and move away?

Away? Away to where?
I find guys everywhere

>Soon people will say, "Look, look"
>She's in that *Guinness Records* book

I'll find a way—can't take this anymore
Goodbye, farewell—I'm heading out the door

>The door! Oh, look who just walked in
>That's him! That's him!—The **Perfect 10!!**

Disclaimer

I've shared stories of my *ten* husbands. However, I have actually been married for more than *fifty* years—to only *one* husband!

But yet, when I think about it . . . that man at my dining table, that man in my bed is *not* the same man I married more than five decades ago.

He doesn't look the same. He doesn't move the same.

He doesn't always act the same.

Yet, he still has those qualities that originally attracted me: Kind, smart, funny, creative, responsible, hard-working.

But, I've learned other things about him:

He's stubborn, opinionated, and a packrat.

So, now I'm wondering: Have I actually been married to several different husbands over the years? Could it be *ten*?!

Oh, well, it really doesn't matter. I just know that my current husband is my "Perfect 10!"

PLAYING

The Dating Game

Truth in Advertising

Attractive female, loves to dress in style, enjoys shopping at exclusive stores for latest fashions and accessories.

> Seeks very wealthy man who would love to show off an attractive, gorgeously-dressed wife at fine restaurants, resorts, and cruises.

Handsome, athletic guy loves watching all types of sports on TV with his buddies.

> Seeks sexy young female with background as waitress and/or barmaid, especially skilled at serving beer.

Handsome gentleman with amazing, extensive list of accomplishments, including, but certainly not limited to, worldwide travels, business dealings, philanthropic good deeds, educational degrees, etc., etc., etc.

> Seeks attractive, quiet, good listener.

Birdbrains

I was watching this nature show on TV about the mating habits of birds. It was really interesting.

There was the male peacock, spreading those gorgeous tail feathers, strutting and prancing all around in front of the female.

Hey, did I tell you about the new guy who showed up at the club last night? Whoa! Did he look *good* in those tight-fittin' jeans. Think I'll go back and try to meet him.

Oh, yeah—back to the nature show. Male penguins tried to impress potential mates by bringing little pebbles and dropping them down in front of the females.

Oh, I almost forgot to ask you: Have you seen the engagement ring that Lisa got from her boyfriend? Wow! That "rock" is *huge*!

Sorry, back to the bird habits. The bowerbird builds this elaborate structure and decorates it with lots of colorful objects. I guess the female chooses the fanciest "love nest."

Wow! Have you heard about the house that Jenny and her fiancé will be moving into after their wedding? It's amazing! Looks almost like a mansion!

> Also on this nature show were several birds that went on and on and on with their "love songs." It seemed like hours and hours! I wonder if birds get laryngitis? Ha, ha!

Oh, I heard the sweetest story about Eric. He really likes that new girl he's dating. Guess what? He wrote a song for her and sang it and played it on his guitar.

Lovesick

Wow! She must be "The One." I've never felt like this before.

> Heart racing, stomach rumbling, headache, feverish. I guess that's how "Lovesick" feels!

That cute, sweet, sexy girl invited me over to her place and made a home-cooked meal just for me.

> She had candles, flowers, pretty napkins, and soft music in the background. Then she brought out her special dish with a proud "Ta Da" as she lifted the lid.

She put only a little food on her own plate—she said she was "watching her figure" (I certainly was!) I ate that large portion she put on my plate and then took an extra helping because she insisted.

> Wait! I've been thinking I'm "Lovesick."

Oh, no! I'm "Sick Sick!"

Wasted Hours?

Hey, girls—remember the hours we spent trying on clothes, wanting to have just the right outfits to wear on our dates?

(Guys dreamt of getting us out of those clothes.)

Hours were spent in front of the mirror trying to decide which hairstyle was most flattering.

(Guys wanted to run their fingers through our hair, leaving us with that "tousled" look.)

Hours were spent applying makeup and choosing just the perfect shade of lipstick.

(Guys had no idea about lipstick shades but would love to smear that lipstick with *hot, passionate* kisses.)

Hour and hours and hours!
Wasted hours??

Don't Tell Sis

Don't tell my sister about your love life. I did. I told her I was more mature now and looking for real, lasting love. I asked her if she could advise me.

> I said I no longer cared so much about looks
> and social position.
> I wanted lasting qualities: Loyal, kind, giving, and
> appreciative—not a complainer.

I wanted someone who was caring, hardworking, protective—a great companion, playful, a snuggler. Someone who would love me unconditionally and do anything for me.

> Did she have any suggestions? Well, she found
> me an answer.
> Come meet Buddy, my new dog! Sis said it'll take
> longer to find a man.

Warning Labels

Some guys and gals should come with warning labels!
(like those we see on drugs and medication)

Warning, may cause:

> Rapid heartbeat
> Dizziness
> Shortness of breath
> Dry mouth
> Insomnia
> Inability to speak coherently
> Anxiety
> Confusion
> Tingling sensations

Warning:

> Beware of serious, long-lasting side effects.
> May become habit-forming.
> Could lead to lifelong dependency.

Wise Man's Advice

Why do I keep falling in love with so many guys?
My head's full of questions—why, why, why's

> Why do I fall for every handsome man I see?
> Why do I believe every line they hand to me?

I decided to consult a master, the sage upon the hill
That expert will have answers. Yes, I'm sure he will

> I grabbed my walking stick and new hiking shoes
>   I'd bought
> It's worth the strenuous climb ahead. (Well, that's
>   what I thought)

I finally found the Wise Man—he was really quite a sight
Sitting there cross-legged, his beard so long and white

> He asked, "What is your problem, my dear?"
> And motioned me closer so that he could hear

I told him I had really tried to be resolute
But then I'd see a fellow who was just so very cute!

> When I'd meet a gentleman who exuded all
>   that charm
> I would figure, *Now surely, there could be no harm.*

And when a manly "hunk" walked through the door
That's when I'd tell myself, "Let's try just one more."

    The astrologer assured me that when the stars align,
    I could be certain that a man would be just fine

There was always another fellow—well, bless my soul!
I realized that things were totally out of control

    Why am I still looking? Why do I persist?
    Am I trying to fulfill some crazy "wish list"?

I said, "Oh, Wise One, please help. Your advice I will heed"
His response—"My dear, it is willpower that you need!"

A Warning for Guys

Look out, fellas, 'cause here we come
We're gonna have you on the run

> We're getting ready; soon it will be that day
> When we're the hunters—you, the prey

Our preparations are not meek and mild
No camouflage for us; we dress to be wild

> Slinky, sparkly, sexy, and sleek
> Catching your eye is what we seek

Next, we'll put on "war paint"
So subtle and ladylike—it ain't

> Lipstick dark red and mascara so black
> Do an extra layer—oh, what the heck!

Let this be your warning to give you a head start
'Cause in the Battle of the Sexes, you're really not that smart

> Yes, we, the fairer sex, can be tough as nails
> When heading out to get you, hot on your trails

We've been waiting—year after year
Now, finally, our time is drawing near

Very near, as a matter of fact
My sisters and I are ready to act

Ready to seek, ready to capture
We know exactly what we are after

Members of the male sex, used to being the pursuer
But now—aha!—you will find that you're . . .

The ones being hunted, the ones being sought
Know what we'll do after you're caught?

We'll remind you of that long-forgotten rule
The one you learned way back in school

That February 29th, the Leap Year Day,
Is also Sadie Hawkins—when all girls may . . .

Ask the boys out!

Love and . . .

"All you need is love"
Beautiful lyrics? Oh, yes!
Realistic? No!

You need love and . . . food
A place to live, furniture
A vehicle for transportation

Clothing, medicines
A way to pay for utilities
Insurance, bills

On and on and on
However, remember that
Love's the most important

Merry-Go-Round

Stop this crazy merry-go-round
I need to get off
It's been guy after guy after guy after guy

    Dating—a total disaster
    I went looking for Mr. Right
    I found Mr. Wrong! Wrong! Wrong!
    I'm done with dating
    Finished with fellas
    Given up on guys
    Suspended all suitors
    Banished boyfriends
    Ditched the dudes

My plan now is to hop off this merry-go-round
Find some "No Man Land," a place minus males
And just be an old maid for the rest of my life or . . .

Go live in a convent
    (Would they take me?)
Become a member of an all-girl band
    (I'd have to learn an instrument)
Sit in my rocking chair all day, crocheting doilies
    (I'd have to learn that, too)

Write my memoir
    (Oh, the tales I could tell!)
Get a dog or cat
    (Okay, *it* could be a male)

Well, as you can see, there are lots of possibilities
But, wait! Maybe I won't have to use any of them
Look who just walked in the door!
It appears to be "Mr. Right, Mr. Handsome, Perfect 10"
All rolled into one!
I'm going to get back on that merry-go-round
And give it *one more whirl*!

Dream to Nightmare

My dream—every young girl's dream:

> That someday my prince will come, handsome,
>   dashing
> Ready to carry me off to his castle
> Where I'll be Princess *and* Belle of the Ball!

My nightmare—when my prince comes:

> I'll be out shopping (perhaps for a ball gown) or
> I'll be having a *really* bad-hair day or
> I'll be out on a date with a "commoner"

Once Upon a Time

Once upon a time life seemed so simple
I believed that dreams really do come true
I'd grow up and meet my beau
Life would then progress just so
That was before you!

> You came along and stole my heart
> Tore my world apart

My knight would ride in upon his steed
And fulfill my every need
He would take me by the hand
My every wish—his command

> But you drove up in your ol' pickup truck
> You laid on the horn, never came to the door

He would dress with stylish taste
Perfectly groomed, not a hair out of place
So mannerly, such wit and charm
As we'd go walking arm in arm

> Well, T-shirts and jeans are your usual wear
> And a baseball cap covers most of your hair

His tastes would be so refined
Candlelit dinners, sipping fine wine
Moonlight strolls along the beach
Nights at the opera and symphony

> It's pizza and beer again for Saturday night
> Then take in a movie or the TV fight

Everything made perfect sense
A pretty little cottage, the white picket fence
Flower gardens in the yard
Our life together, a picture postcard

> So, why am I here in a one-bedroom flat
> No sign of a yard, just a few potted plants?

Once upon a time, I believed in fairy tales
Knights in shining armor, screen idols, too
But then . . . I found *you*
(And I'm so glad I did!)

Beginnings

Where did you meet your true love?

We met on a cruise ship—
Our "*Love* Boat"

We met at a garden shop—
Love blossomed

We met at the airport—
Love took flight

We met at the coffee shop—
Love brewed

We met at the tailor shop—
Our *Love*—a perfect fit

We met at Niagara Falls—
And fell in *Love*

We met at the pharmacy—
Love cures all ills

We met at a concert—
Made *Love*ly music together

We met flying kites at the park—
Love soared

We met at a neighborhood bar—
    And soon were drunk on *Love*

We met at a baseball game—
    Our *Love* was a home run

We met at a church service—
    Our *Love*—heaven sent

Husband's Revisions

I thought I'd share **"Beginnings"** with my husband,
  But, as you can see,
    He started to add his own "revisions."

We met on a cruise ship—
    Our "*Love* Boat" . . . . **capsized**

We met at a garden shop—
    Love blossomed . . . . **root rot**

We met at the airport—
    Love took flight . . . . **turbulence**

Hey, stop it! That's not funny.
    (Well, actually, it kinda is!)

"TYING THE KNOT"

and Beyond

The Fine Print

Guess I didn't read the fine print (on our marriage vows).

For richer or poorer
I don't recall reading about . . .

    Living paycheck to paycheck

    Borrowing from Peter to pay Paul

    The old car held together with duct tape

    A tiny apartment with borrowed furniture

In sickness and in health
I didn't expect to have . . .

    All family members sick at the same time

    Trips to the emergency room

    Medicines, prescriptions

    Doctor bills to pay

For better or worse
The "fine print" should remind us to look back at our years of marriage and realize we overcame challenges, grew stronger, and enjoyed countless blessings along the way.

For "better or worse"? My life has definitely been made **better** by sharing it with you!

May I Have This Dance?

May I have this dance? Will you be my permanent partner?
Make it our dance for all the years of our lives?

> Beginning with the wedding waltz
> Continuing on and on and on
> Because marriage is its own dance
> A dance with ever-changing movements

Together, holding each other so closely
But then moving farther apart, needing some space

> Sometimes one of us leads, sometimes the other
> I supporting you, and then you supporting me

Moving forward with our lives, then stepping back
Faster, and then slower

> Alone, just us as a couple
> Joining with others in celebration

Sometimes all awhirl, with people, events, places
Spinning in our heads
Other times moving slowly, with time to contemplate, savor,
hold closer, cherish

But always, it will be you and I together
Loving and caring for each other in our
marriage dance
Please be my partner

How to Get Your Honey to Do Your Honey-Do's

"Oh, Honey (or 'Dear' or 'Sweetie' or 'Babe')"
Any "pet name" is always a good way to start!

One plan—Stress positive outcomes gained by working on the list. "Oh, Honey—did you see that magazine article about building great muscles by simply doing ordinary household tasks? Guess what? One of the best exercises is moving boxes to the attic.
Yes, amazing results!"

Another ploy—"Oh, Honey, guess what Phyllis told me? She heard that new neighbor across the street (the cute little blonde) talking about how good-looking you are. Well, I'm a little jealous, but also a little proud. So, I say, just go ahead and let her get a good look at my 'Handsome Hubby' while you're mowing the front lawn."

Here's another—"Oh, Honey, I'm so sorry to mention this now, but, it's just so hard for me to get into a romantic mood when I'm hearing that *drip, drip, drip* from a leaky bathroom faucet in the background. Do you suppose you could fix that naughty ol' faucet?

I'll be waiting right here for you to hurry back to bed."

There you go—boxes moved, lawn mowed, and faucet repaired—all thanks to my Handy Dandy "How To" Instructions!

What Happened?

Hey, honey, what happened to that
Cute, little shapely gal I married back when?

    Oh, I guess she ran off with that
    Handsome dude I married, the one with
    Dark, wavy hair and six-pack abs.

Yep, I guess that must be it.
Well, I say, let's just let them go. Good riddance.

    Yes, I agree, 'cause now we have each other.
    Fun, caring, comfortable together.

Oh, I do love you, dear!
Yes, I love you, too!

Whispers

I have a confession to make.

When I whispered "sweet nothings" in my husband's ears,
That's exactly what some of them were—"nothings."
Why? Because he couldn't hear them.

My hubby has a hearing loss, but today . . .
Oh, no! He came home with hearing aids.

Now, instead of trying to memorize items
to include on my shopping list or
rehearsing that presentation for my club meeting,
I'll need to make sure that my whispers are actually
sweet words of affection for my husband
and *not* those ol' "sweet nothings" as in the past.
Because, now, he can hear what I say!

Hidden Secrets

Oh, my dear, sweet wife
There's shocking news of your past.
Tell me—who are you?

> I'm the wife you wed,
> Though my past does haunt me still.
> Please, help me forget.

No, I don't know you.
You keep dark secrets from me
That I can't understand.

> Listen, listen. Please.
> That girl with the checkered past
> Is just that—the past.

Then why not tell me?
Wasn't it my right to know?
We need honesty in our marriage.

> I was so afraid
> That you'd not want me if you knew
> And I just loved you so much.

Questions:

What is the shocking secret?
Was she wrong to hide it from him?
Can he forgive . . . and forget?
Will love survive?

Our Gala Event

Whoo! Hoo! Guess where we could go for New Year's Eve?
That special, fancy gala at the big hotel downtown.
What do you think? It's pretty pricey, but it will be
really "high class."

You'd get to look handsome and debonair in your tuxedo.
I'd wear my sexy, sparkly dress and those shiny, strappy
high heels.
We haven't been all dressed up like that in a long time.

There will be amazing decorations, live music for dancing,
Fancy hors d'oeuvres and fine champagne.

We'd get to rub elbows with "everybody who's anybody,"
as they say.
What do you think, honey?

Truthfully, I'd like to get rid of that tux. Give it to a
poor, needy penguin.
I know. Those sexy high heels . . . My feet hurt just
looking at them.

I'd rather skip that "fancy-pants" event. But, if you
really want, I'll go.
Yeah, same here.

So, what do you think?
No! (in unison)

We'll put on some comfy clothes, make a big bowl of popcorn, and settle on the couch for a good movie. At midnight, we can open a bottle of champagne, get out those hats and noisemakers from the party store, watch the countdown on TV, and, of course, share a big kiss or two.

Sounds great! But, you *know* how we sometimes fall asleep watching television, so we'd better set an alarm. Yep, I think we have great plans for *our* Gala Event!

But

As newlyweds, we had dreams of fun adventures,
adventures that were postponed, due to having our children.

We haven't gone on all those ocean cruises, but . . .
We've had lots of "splashy fun" at bath time.

We haven't had seats to the World Series, but . . .
We've watched some very exciting Little League games.

We haven't gone to the famous Bolshoi Ballet, but . . .
We've been proud parents at local dance recitals.

We haven't seen the mighty pyramids of Egypt, but . . .
We've helped build impressive sand castles at the beach.

We haven't tracked wildlife on an African safari, but . . .
We've watched caravans of ants at work and baby birds
in their nests.

We haven't seen the Northern Lights, Aurora Borealis, but . . .
We've seen the excitement when a child first spies a
rainbow or finds the Big Dipper.

We haven't eaten French cuisine at a Parisian cafe, but . . . We've savored delicious carrots grown from seeds in a child's own garden.

We haven't attended a big Broadway production, but . . . We've shared enjoyable evenings at our local community theater.

When the children are all grown, we'll just pick up— and dust off—those postponed dreams from long ago.

And here is the beauty of it all . . .

We can still experience many of our dream adventures. In addition, we have—to treasure forever—beautiful memories of wonderful adventures shared with our children.

Joys of Growing Old Together

Joys of growing old together: **Time, Comfort, Memories**
We've earned them. Let's enjoy them.

Time

To look forward and look back, put in perspective
To retrieve, reflect, resolve

To clean house, both literally and figuratively
Assess the value of what we have in our lives
Let some things go, so we can hold others more closely

To keep or discard
We toss things up—those of value settle back down
to be kept, valued, treasured
The rest of that "stuff"—poor decisions, regrets, dreams
unfulfilled, detours taken—can be tossed to the winds
to be carried away

Let bygones be bygones. Say "Bye" and let it go.

Comfort

To know we can really be ourselves with each other
To feel comfortable, accepted, and appreciated just as we are

It's true. We can almost read each other's minds, better
understand the other's moods, anticipate and fulfill needs

Yes, "old married folk" can, and do, start finishing each other's sentences.

("That guy on TV, doesn't he remind you of . . . Yeah, that fellow we met on that trip . . . Oh, right, we sat there eating lunch with him . . . yes, near that big waterfall . . .")

Hang around the house in our "ol' comfy clothes." Make a bowl of popcorn and settle onto the couch to watch a movie together. That can qualify as an enjoyable evening. (Old Folks Date Night!)

Memories

To reach back and recall
To remember people and events from the past
Find memories in albums, in drawers, in our minds
Bring some from the back burner to put out in front
Call an old friend; enjoy a voice from the past

Some memories may be wistful and bittersweet,
But most will give us smiles, laughter, and happy tears,
Allowing us to visit once again and relive those special times

To vow that, in our remaining years, we will make more precious memories to share—many more!

Gratitude

Along with the **Joys** we share of **Time, Comfort, and Memories**,

let us not forget to also share **Gratitude**

Gratitude for the sanctuary that we have built together—

a sanctuary from the outside world

where we can feel safe and secure in each other's arms

Our Road

Marriage—Hands joined, hearts joined, lives joined
Ready to travel down *Our Road* together

> The road we thought was all mapped out—
> marriage and careers
> home and family
> retirement and travel
> All mapped out. Ha! Ha!

The actual road—
starts and stops
twists and turns
ruts and roadblocks
Steps and missteps
Adventures and misadventures
Dreams dreamt and dreams dissolved

> Yet, in spite of all these stumbles and detours
> Here we are—still cruising down *Our Road* together

I Love Thee

How do I love thee? Ah, that age-old question!
First, *why* do I love thee? Well, let me count the ways

1 ♥ You've seen me at my best and seen me at my worst
       Thank you for choosing to remember my best

2 ♥ You've helped me weather difficult times with your
       sense of humor. You've known when to provide
       a smile, a chuckle, or a good ol' hearty belly laugh
       just when I needed it most

3 ♥ In times of sadness and sorrow, you've let me
       cry on your shoulder or let me go off to cry all alone
       You always seemed to know which one I needed to do

4 ♥ You've stuck with me through thick and thin—
       More accurately, through thin and thick
       Yes, there's a lot more "thick" now, especially
          around my middle
       But, kindly, you don't mention it

5 ♥ You've let me tell you all my crazy dreams, and, then,
       when I need it most, you've helped me wake up
          to reality
       Thanks for letting me enjoy the ride before you
          burst the bubble

6 ♥ When I've felt down, so unsure of myself, you lifted
me up—

sometimes, even put me on a pedestal
How special you can make me feel!

7 ♥ We've shared good times and bad

I appreciate that you seem to write the good times in
large, bold print on your mental list
and the bad times in small, faint letters—
sometimes even in disappearing ink

8 ♥ Our relationship has grown stronger over the years

You've reminded me of this as we shared wonderful
memories
envisioning dreams for many more years to come

These are some of the many reasons *why* I love thee.
Now, back to that famous question: *How* do I love thee?

My answer—by trying to be as kind, caring,
and loving to you
as you have been to me during our many
years together!

MORE THOUGHTS

on Love

Flowers—Symbols of Love

A prom corsage, worn by a girl in her special dress
To that memorable high school dance

> A wedding bouquet carried by a blushing,
>   misty-eyed bride
> As she walks down the aisle

Dandelion "bouquet" clutched in a child's tiny fist
A special gift for Mom

> Long-stem roses, a gift to a wife
> Celebrating a special anniversary

Garden flowers lovingly tended by an elderly couple
Enjoyed from a porch swing

Confucius Say

Opposites Attract
Wise Old Saying Very True
I'm Right, and You're Wrong

> Tiny Band of Gold
> So Gently Slipped on Finger
> Life-Changing Action

Have Lovesick Symptoms
Racing Heartbeat, Breathlessness
Please Don't Call Doctor

> Love Grows, It's a Fact
> One and One Join to Marry
> And Baby Makes Three

Math So Very Strange
Explain How Two Become One
Then Baby Makes Three

Confucius Say

"Lovesick" Symptoms End
Now to Develop Into
A Strong "Mature Love"

For "Marital Bliss"
So Much Hard Work to Achieve
Enjoy Sweet Reward!

Is Said "Give and Take
Secret to Happy Marriage"
One More Secret—*Love!*

Dating Attributes
Face, Shape, But More Important . . .
Good Ears—Listening!

Confucius Say

In marriage, build home
Providing sanctuary
From the outside world

Sharing hopes and dreams
Helps our love to grow stronger
Seeking fulfillment

Working as a team
Working to fulfill our dreams
Making our house—Home

Husband arrives late
Meal on table growing cold
Prays for good excuse

Adding of children
Brings much joy and happiness
Also, exhaustion!

Confucius Say

Heart racing, tongue-tied
"Doctor, diagnosis, please"
"Infatuation!"

Cupid has bad aim
I asked for a Mr. Right
This is Mr. Wrong!

Hey, Cupid, what's wrong?
I'm still waiting for my man
Asleep on the job?

House becomes a Home
When filled with Family, Friends
Memories, and Love

May I have this dance?
Wedding waltz, then on and on . . .
Marriage *Is* the dance

IN APPRECIATION

*T*hanks to CelenaDiana Bumpus and her "Poets in Motion" Writing Group for helping me learn more about types of poetry, sharing some amazing examples, and always offering supportive feedback.

Thanks to Members of my Toastmasters Clubs for listening to the "Interpretive Reading" of my work, sharing helpful evaluation comments, and providing so many opportunities for creative growth over the years.

Thanks to Sheryl Roush for allowing me to be a "published author" when she included my writing in three of her wonderful *Heart Book* Series.

ABOUT THE AUTHOR

*C*onnie Jameson, a retired teacher, lives in Southern California. She is a wife of more than fifty-five years, mother, grandmother and great-grandmother.

Among Connie's interests are reading, travel, nature and theater. Connie enjoys finding the "wit and wisdom" in every day, real-life experiences. She is currently working on an illustrated children's book.

Made in the USA
Las Vegas, NV
15 February 2022

43953392R00049